Table of Contents

While there are whole schools of thought on cooking steak grilling evangelist Meathead Goldwyn pushes the reverse sear method, for example chicken, for whatever reason, hasn't inspired the same fervor. No one gets as excited about it. But according to the chefs we talked to, chicken is actually much harder to cook than steak. "Chicken is one of the most unforgiving types of meat," says chef Jon Sloan, the culinary director at Crack Shack. "Unlike beef, it doesn't have any connected tissue or fat collagen, with the exception of the thigh." Because of chicken's lower fat content, you have to nail the cooking times and technique exactly or else you'll end up with dry, stringy meat. Furthermore, chicken needs to be fully cooked to 165 degrees due to salmonella concerns your move, chicken sashimi unlike steak, which can be finished rare. This can make it harder to get a juicy piece of chicken, Angelo Auriana, the chef at Officine BRERA, points out. . For those who do prefer chicken breasts, butterflying them is the best way to cook them, according to Wilschke. The technique, which refers to splitting open a piece of meat horizontally and then opening it like a book, creates an even thickness for a breast that's otherwise wedge-shaped, which makes for even cooking. Alternatively, you can use a meat hammer to even out the meat, Wilschke recommends. Here's how to do that, from executive chef Michael Kornick, of Marshall's Landing: "Trim the rib meat, gently pound the fattest part of the muscle with the side of the mallet with teeth or points. This will break down the tissue a bit. Then use the smooth side to even out the muscle." (These directions are for skinless breasts specifically; if keeping the skin on, Kornick recommends cutting off the tenders from the breasts, and pan frying them separately.) Roasting chicken whole and skin-on is probably the absolute best way to preserve flavor and moisture, Wilschke says as long as you truss it well, so that the meat doesn't dry out. For the purposes of this book, however, we're focusing on chicken cookbook for beginners.

Buying Previously Frozen Meat.

We're going for juicy chicken, and juiciness comes from locking in water content. When chicken, or any meat, is previously frozen, this can dry it out. Look for the "fresh, never frozen" label on packaged chicken, but sometimes you can't even trust that, says James Wilschke, the executive chef at Filifera in Hollywood. "I'm sure there are grocery stores that are overstocked on product and if they don't want it to spoil, they might freeze it to just extend the life of it," he says. There are probably higher end brands of poultry that you can trust, but he recommends checking with your butcher at the meat case just to be safe.

Buying Chicken That Is Brine-Injected Or Has Added Water.

That's according to Sloan. We know, this seems like a paradox because we just said that water was important for juicy chicken, but brine-injected chicken can actually have compromised texture and flavor, because the industrial brining helps mask deficiencies in both. It's much better to purchase a higher quality of chicken, if your wallet allows. Sloan also recommends staying away from chicken with added dyes. "I think it's important to use chickens with non-GMO feed and that are pasture raised 'free-range' is meaningless," says. "The diet is what makes the chicken taste a certain way and texture."

Passing Up Bone-In Chicken Thighs. (Boneless Breasts May Be The Hardest To Get Right.)

Boneless chicken breasts may be the least intimidating for cooks who don't want to deal with bones, but they're also the hardest to get right, according to some chefs. "The breast is one of the most difficult [cuts] to cook," Sloan says. Chef Aaron Robins of Boneyard Bistro in Los Angeles disagrees, kind of. "[Thighs] will come out the moistest," he says, "but cooking a boneless, skinless, butterflied breast cutlet will cook evenly and quickly." In a way, they both seem to be driving at the same conclusion. Even though cooking chicken breasts is more straightforward than cooking bone-in thighs which take longer to cook and are asymmetrical, potentially complicating cooking the latter are actually more forgiving, Sloan asserts. In other words, you can vary the cooking time by a minute or two on a bone-in thigh and still end up with a pretty juicy piece of meat because of the way the bone helps the meat retain moisture. "There's fat in the bone that's going to melt and keep the meat moist, and it'll also provide a lot more flavor," Wilschke says.   Craig Hopson, executive chef at Farmhouse in Los Angeles, affirms that chicken thighs are best for newbie cooks. "They are the least likely to dry out, and they are also the most flavorful cuts on their own," he says for a wealth of roasting recipes, go here.

Forgetting To Dry Your Meat In The Fridge.

This step sounds kind of contradictory. We want juicy meat, right, So why do we dry it and take moisture out of it, Well, we want the inside to be juicy, but we want that lovely caramelized crust on the outside and we can get both when we brine first, and then dry it. "People want to get really crispy meat, and the general rule of cooking is moisture is the enemy of caramelization," Wilschke says. "When you want to get meat crispy, you want the skin as dry as possible." He recommends air drying the meat out of the package in the fridge for up to four hours, and then patting it down with a clean paper towel to soak up any remaining moisture. "You can even have it air dry in your refrigerator for a day or two if you want," he says. "That's a trick for my fried chicken. I'll bread the chicken the night before, and the flour is going to soak up a lot of that moisture from the meat, and it allows for a lot crisper of a crust."

Starting With Cold Meat.

Just like with cooking steak, you don't want to start with an ice cold piece of meat fresh out of the fridge, Wilschke says. This can lead to overcooking and uneven cooking. "A lot of chefs will temper their meat," he explains, letting it come to room temperature over an extended period of time. While Robins recommends taking it out 20 to 30 minutes before cooking, Wilschke advocates for longer. "The meat can sit on the countertop for a couple of hours, up to four hours," he says. "It won't go bad, nothing is going to happen in that four hours. If you throw an ice cold piece of chicken in a pan, the outside's going to get dried out by the time the inside is cooked fully." Make sure to give it another pat dry with a paper towel before you drop it in the pan.

Not Getting The Pan Hot Enough.

Drizzle some canola or coconut oil in a pan and turn it up to super high heat, Wilschke advises. (Avoid butter here; if you want to add it, add it at the basting step mentioned in the next paragraph.) High temperature is important to get a nice sear and caramelization. Avoid using extra virgin olive oil, which has a lower smoking point and will start smoking by the time your pan gets hot enough, Wilschke says. Next, lay your piece of chicken skin side down. After about eight to nine minutes on one side for your average bone-in thigh obviously that estimate varies flip it once. Then lower your heat to medium, Wilschke suggests. Robins agrees. For extra juiciness, add some fat a pad of butter, more oil when you flip your chicken and baste it, spooning the fat over the still cooking chicken. This will make for a moister final product.

Last But Not Least: Not Letting The Meat Rest

When it's finished cooking, just like a good steak, chicken needs to rest. "Once you have hit 165 degrees, stop the heat and let it rest for few minutes before cutting, so the juices redistribute themselves back through the meat," Robins says. As chef Ryan Prentiss described with steak, this process allows for the collagen in the meat to thicken the juices, resulting in the moistest possible piece of meat.

Recipe

Lemon Chicken

Ingredients

• 2 boneless skinless chicken breast

• 1 large egg (beaten)

• neutral-flavored oil (vegetable, canola, etc) (for deep frying)

• Marinade:

• 1½ tsp soy sauce

- ½ tsp sesame oil (roasted)

- 1 Tbsp potato starch/cornstarch

- 1 tsp sake (Chinese cooking wine or sherry)

- Coating:

- ¼ cup all-purpose flour (plain flour)

- ¼ cup potato starch/cornstarch

- 1 tsp baking soda

Sauce:

- 6 Tbsp lemon juice (6 Tbsp = 3 lemons)

- 4 Tbsp plum sauce

- 4 tsp sugar

- ⅓ cup water

- 1 tsp potato starch/cornstarch

- Pinch kosher/sea salt (use half for table salt) (to taste)

Instructions

- Cut the chicken breast in half (I did this so the chicken will cook faster) and marinate with all the ingredients for Marinade for 30 minutes.

- Mix and then sift all the ingredients for the Coating and set aside.

• Mix all the ingredients for the Sauce in a small saucepan. Heat the saucepan over medium to low heat. Stir the Sauce to blend well. Once the Sauce starts to bubble and boil, reduce heat and stirring occasionally until the Sauce becomes thicker. Remove the saucepan from the heat and set aside. Note: As the recipe suggested, I made the double amount of sauce. The recipe here is already doubled the original recipe. I also adjusted to add more corn starch and reduce the amount of water compared to the original recipe.

• Dip the chicken in the egg, and then dust with the Coating evenly. Shake off the excess Coating.

• Heat 2-3 inches of the oil in a wok to 350F for deep frying (How To Deep Fry Food). Gently drop the chicken into the oil.

• Deep fry the chicken to a light golden brown. Drain the excess oil by laying the chicken on a dish lined with paper towels.

• Cut the chicken into pieces. Drizzle the Sauce on top and serve immediately.

Ingredients

Chicken

• 2 (~8-ounce) chicken breasts (pasture raised, organic when possible, boneless and skinless)

• 1 ½ tsp avocado oil (or other neutral oil with high smoke point)

• 1 ½ Tbsp apple cider vinegar

• 1/2 tsp sea salt

• 1/4 tsp black pepper

• 1 tsp dried oregano (or sub 2 tsp fresh)

• 1 tsp dried basil (or sub 2 tsp fresh)

• 1 tsp smoked paprika

• 1/8 tsp red pepper flake (reduce or omit for less heat)

• 1 Tbsp fresh chopped rosemary

• 1 dash cayenne pepper (optional // reduce or omit for less heat)

Tahini Dressing

• Parsley

• Brown Rice, White Rice, Quinoa, or Cauliflower Rice

Instructions

• If using grill, start by heating grill. If using a grill pan, set on the stovetop and lightly oil.

• Optional: For quicker cooking, place chicken breasts between two pieces of parchment paper and use the underside of a saucepan to gently pound the meat into thinner pieces. This can cut cook time in half.

• Add chicken to a shallow bowl or dish and top with oil and vinegar, then flip 1-2 times to coat.

• Add half of the spices to one side of the breasts and half of the spices to the other side. Mixture will include sea salt, pepper, oregano, basil, paprika, pepper flake, rosemary, and cayenne (optional). Flip a few times to coat.

• Let marinate for at least 15 minutes or overnight (covered in the refrigerator // can marinate up to 24 hours).

How To Roast A Chicken

Ingredients

• One chicken, 3 to 4 lbs.

• Kosher salt

• Freshly cracked black pepper

• Pad of butter, optional

• Squeeze of lemon, optional

Instructions

• A day before (or at least 2 to 3 hours before) you plan on roasting the chicken place it in a large bowl (4-qt or so). Season it all over with kosher salt using about 1 teaspoon for every pound of meat. Cover the bowl and stick it in the fridge. Remove bowl from fridge an hour (if possible) before you plan on roasting the chicken.

• Preheat the oven to 475°F. Choose a shallow oven-safe skillet. Preheat the pan over medium heat for about five minutes. Wipe the chicken dry (very dry!). Season all over with pepper if you wish. Set it breast side up in the pan. It should sizzle.

• Place the chicken in the pan in the center of the oven for 25 minutes. Turn the bird over — drying the bird and preheating the pan should keep the skin from sticking. Roast for another 10 minutes, then flip back over to re-crisp the breast skin, another 5 to 10 minutes. If you have an instant-read thermometer, it should register about 165°F.

• Remove the chicken from the oven and turn off
the heat. Lift the chicken from the roasting pan and
set on a plate. Add about a tablespoon or two of
water to the hot pan and swirl it. Slash the stretched
skin between the thighs and breasts of the chicken,
then tilt the bird and plate over the roasting pan to
drain the juice into the drippings. Add a pad (a
tablespoon or so) of butter to the pan, if you wish.
Using a wooden spoon, scrape up any chicken bits
stuck to the pan. Taste the sauce. Add a squeeze of
lemon if you wish.

• Let the chicken rest 15 minutes before carving it.
Serve with the sauce on the side.

• To make a stock with the carcass, remove any
remaining meat from the bones. Be sure to really
get into the breast and backbone and extract any
meat. Save this meat for a salad or soup. Place all of
the bones in a 4-qt pot and cover with water.
Simmer slowly for about 2 to 3 hours. Strain into a
bowl. Transfer stock to quart containers and store in
the fridge for a week or the freezer for up to 6

months. You should have about 1.5 to 2 quarts of stock.

Last Minute Chicken

Ingredients

- 2 tsp garlic powder

- 1 1/2 tsp onion powder

- 2 tsp paprika OR smoked paprika

- 2 tsp dried oregano

- 1 1/2 tsp black pepper

- 1 tsp kosher salt

- 3 lbs. boneless skinless chicken thighs

- 1 tbsp olive oil

- 2 tbsp fresh cilantro, chopped (optional)

- US Customary - Metric

Instructions

- Combine the garlic, onion, paprika, oregano, pepper and salt in a small bowl. Sprinkle half the spices over the chicken. Turn the chicken pieces over and sprinkle the remaining spices over them. Rub the spices into the chicken, if needed, to coat well.

- Grill Pan Directions:

• Heat a nonstick grill pan over medium heat. Drizzle with the olive oil. Place half the chicken in the grill pan, making sure there is a gap between the pieces. Cook the chicken without touching it for 5 minutes. Flip the pieces over and cook for 3 to 5 minutes until they're cooked through. Repeat with remaining chicken.

• Broiling Directions:

• Preheat oven to broil.

• Place an oven rack 6 inches from the top of the oven. Put a wire rack over a large baking tray and arrange the chicken on the wire rack. Place the chicken in the oven and broil for 6 minutes. Remove the chicken from the oven, turn each piece of chicken over, and then broil for 5 to 6 minutes.

• Let the cooked chicken rest for 5 minutes before serving. Sprinkle the pieces with cilantro, if desired.

The Best Clay Pot Chicken Rice

Ingredients

For the rice

• 1 cup (230 grams) raw white rice (short round) (*see footnote 1)

• 350 milliliters water (about 1 and 1/2 cup)

• 2 teaspoons vegetable oil

• 15 (20 grams / 0.5 ounces) dried shiitake mushrooms (or 2 cups fresh shiitake mushrooms)

• For marinade

• 2 (500 grams / 1 pound) bone-in chicken leg-and-thigh portions , chopped (*see footnote 2) or 4 boneless chicken thighs

• 1 tablespoon light soy sauce

• 1 tablespoon Shaoxing wine (or Japanese sake)

• 1 teaspoon ginger , minced

• 1 teaspoon sugar

• 1/2 teaspoon salt

• 1 tablespoon cornstarch

• For the sauce

• 3 cloves garlic , crushed

• 4 tablespoons oyster sauce

• 2 teaspoons sugar

• 2 cups Chinese broccoli, baby bok choy or chopped broccoli (Optional)

Instructions

For the Prep

• Rinse rice a few times and drain. Add water and mix. Let the rice soak for 30 minutes.

• Rinse shiitake mushrooms. Place dried shiitake mushrooms in a medium sized bowl and add warm water to cover. Mix a few times so that the mushrooms are coated with water. Set aside and allow to rehydrate for about 20 minutes. (Slice fresh mushroom if you use it instead.)

• Combine chicken, light soy sauce, Shaoxing wine, ginger, sugar, and salt in a large bowl. Mix well. Blend in cornstarch and mix well by hand until chicken is evenly coated. Marinate at room temperature.

• When the shiitake mushrooms turn soft, carefully rinse mushrooms to remove any dirt. Drain and set aside.

Start Cooking

• Drain rice and add into a medium sized dutch oven (or clay pot). Add 350 milliliters water. Add Heat over medium high heat. Add 1 teaspoon oil and mix well. Bring to a boil while stirring regularly, just like cooking risotto. Turn to medium heat. Continue to cook and stir, until the water is almost absorbed by the rice, about 5 minutes. Cover and simmer over lowest heat for 10 minutes.

• While simmering the rice, cook the chicken and mushrooms. Add the remaining 1 teaspoon of oil into a nonstick skillet over medium high heat until warm. Add chicken and let it cook for 1 minute without stirring. Place the chicken so that you cook the skin side first, until golden brown. Flip and cook the other side until golden brown, and the chicken is half cooked through. Turn to lowest heat. Transfer the chicken to a plate.

• (Optional) Use a spoon to transfer the extra oil to a small bowl, until just a thin layer of oil remains in the skillet. If you use skinless chicken, skip this step.

• Turn back to medium high heat and add shiitake mushrooms. Stir and cook for 2 minutes. Transfer to a plate and set aside.

• When the rice is ready (the water should be fully absorbed by now), arrange chicken, mushrooms, and Chinese broccoli on top of the rice. Cover and continue to simmer for 18-20 minutes (the longer you simmer, the more crispy the rice on the bottom will be). Be careful - you should move as quickly as you can, so the temperature of the rice won't drop too much.

• While the rice is cooking, mix the oyster sauce with the sugar and garlic in a small bowl.

• When the rice is done, remove from heat and uncover. Drizzle oyster sauce on top immediately, while the rice is hot, and mix everything well with a spatula. I suggest you scrape the rice from the bottom while the pot is still warm. Otherwise, it will be a bit difficult to scoop out.

• Serve hot as a main dish/

Gung Bao Chicken

Ingredient

• 1/3 cup unsalted peanuts

• 1 pound (or a little more) boneless, skinless chicken breasts, cut into 3/4-inch (18-mm) cubes

• 1 tablespoon cornstarch

• 4 tablespoon light soy sauce

• 2 tablespoons vegetable or unroasted peanut oil

• 1 teaspoon Szechuan peppercorns

• 2 dried red chilies, roughly chopped or crushed

• 2 garlic cloves, peeled and very thinly sliced

• One (1-inch) knob ginger, peeled and very thinly sliced

• 4 scallions, trimmed and chopped

Directions

• Heat a wok over medium heat. Add the peanuts and gently toast the peanuts, shaking the pan occasionally, until they're a beautiful golden brown, 2 to 3 minutes. Transfer the peanuts to a plate to cool.

• Meanwhile, place the chicken, cornstarch, and half the soy sauce in a large bowl and gently toss until all of the chicken is well coated. Cover and set aside for 10 minutes.

• Heat the wok over medium heat and add the oil. Once the oil is hot, remove the wok from the heat and throw in the Szechuan peppercorns and dried red chilies. Stir continuously 20 to 30 seconds, until the chilies start to turn light brown in color.

• Place the wok over medium-high heat then add the chicken. Fry 2 to 3 minutes, until it just starts to turn golden. Then add the garlic, ginger, scallions, and peanuts. Stir-fry constantly until the chicken is cooked through and tender, 1 to 2 minutes. Pour the remaining soy sauce over the chicken, toss well, and serve immediately.

Orange Chicken Over Rice

Ingredients

For The Orange Sauce:

• 3/4 cup orange juice

• 3 tablespoons soy sauce

• 1 tablespoons sriracha

• 1 tablespoon honey plus more as needed

• 1 teaspoon sesame oil

• ½ teaspoon red pepper flakes

For The Chicken:

• 1 large egg

• 3/4 cup cornstarch

• 1 1/4 pounds boneless skinless chicken thighs or breasts cut into 1-inch pieces

• 1/2 cup canola or other neutral oil

• Salt

• 2 tsp sesame seeds for garnish (optional)

• 1 green onion green parts only, sliced, for garnish

• Cooked white rice for serving

Instructions

• In a small saucepan over medium heat, whisk the orange juice, soy sauce, Sriracha, honey, sesame oil, and red pepper flakes. Bring to a sim¬mer and cook for 6 to 7 min¬utes until slightly thickened (it should lightly coat the back of a spoon). Remove from the heat and set aside, uncovered, for 5 minutes. Taste and if needed to balance flavors, stir in up to 1 1/2 teaspoons honey. You should have about 2/3 cup.

To Make The Chicken:

• In a large bowl, whisk the egg until blended. Place a large bowl next to the egg and put the cornstarch into it.

• Add the chicken to the bowl with the beaten egg and toss to coat. Using a spider or large slotted spoon, lift the chicken from the egg and let any excess drip back into the bowl. Toss the chicken in the cornstarch to coat, shake off any excess cornstarch, and set aside.

• Line a plate or baking sheet with two layers of paper towels and set aside. In a large (12-incskillet over medium-high heat, heat the canola oil. There should be plenty to cover the bottom completely.

• When the skillet is hot, carefully add the chicken to the hot oil. Cook for 3 to 4 minutes on each side, or until golden and crispy. Transfer the chicken to the prepared plate and lightly season with salt. Drain any excess oil and wipe the pan with a paper towel.

• Reheat the skillet over medium heat. Add the chicken, gently cook to reheat. Increase the heat to high, then pour 1/2 cup of orange sauce over the chicken. Stir to coat. Cook for 2 to 3 minutes to heat the sauce through, reduce it and let it adhere to the chicken. If you want more sauce for bigger flavor, add the rest. (If there's leftover sauce, use it to season a broccoli stir-fry. See the Note.)

• Transfer the chicken to a plate and garnish with sesame seeds and green onion. Serve with cooked white rice.

Instant Pot Keto Chicken Thighs In Lemon-Garlic Cream Sauce

Ingredients

• 2 tablespoons vegetable oil

• 4 bone-in, skin-on chicken thighs

• Salt and pepper to taste

• 1/2 medium onion thinly sliced

• 4 cloves garlic minced

• 1/2 cup dry white wine

• 1 cup chicken broth

• 3 tablespoons fresh lemon juice

• 1/2 cup heavy cream

• 1 tablespoon corn starch optional

• 2 tablespoons butter or margarine

• 1/2 teaspoon thyme leaves

• 1/4 teaspoon salt

Instructions

• Turn on a multi-functional pressure cooker (such as Instant Pot(R)) and select Saute function. Heat vegetable oil.

• Season chicken thighs with salt and pepper on both sides; add to Instant Pot(R). Cook one side at a time until both sides of the chicken are a golden brown, 3 to 4 minutes per side. Remove chicken from the pot and set aside.

• Add onion and sauté for 1 minute. Add garlic and cook for 1 more minute. Pour in white wine and stir to scrape brown bits from the bottom of the pot. Stir in chicken broth and lemon juice; bring to a boil and cook until broth has reduced slightly, 2 to 3 minutes. Turn off the Sauté function.

• Return chicken Instant Pot(R). Close and lock the lid. Select High pressure according to manufacturer's instructions; set timer for 10 minutes. Allow 10 to 15 minutes for pressure to build.

• Release pressure using the natural-release method according to manufacturer's instructions, for 10 minutes. Release remaining pressure carefully using the quick-release method, about 5 minutes. Unlock and remove the lid.

• Optional step: Whisk heavy cream and corn starch together in a small bowl if you prefer a thicker sauce (this will add to the net carbs of the meal, but will thicken the sauce). Leave the cream on its own if you prefer lower carbs with a lighter sauce.

• Remove chicken from the pot and set aside. Select the Sauté mode and bring sauce to a boil.

• Whisk in heavy cream, butter or margarine, salt, and thyme. Cook until sauce has thickened slightly, 2 to 3 minutes. Serve chicken drizzled with the sauce.

Kinny Chicken Marsala (Healthy Chicken Marsala)

Ingredients

• 2 large boneless skinless chicken breasts (8 ounces each)

• Kosher salt

• Freshly ground black pepper

• 1/4 cup plus 1 teaspoon all-purpose flour

• 1 tablespoon unsalted butter

- 2 teaspoons olive oil
- 3 garlic cloves minced
- 1/4 cup finely chopped shallots
- 8 ounces sliced cremini mushrooms
- 3 ounces sliced shiitake mushrooms
- 1/3 cup Marsala wine
- 1/2 cup Swanson 88% fat-free chicken broth I used chicken stock since it was all I had on hand
- 2 tablespoons chopped fresh parsley

Instructions

- Preheat the oven to 200°F.
- Slice the chicken breasts in half horizontally to make 4 cutlets. Put each cutlet between two sheets of plastic wrap and lightly pound them until they are about 1/4 inch thick. Season with 1/2 teaspoon salt and a pinch of black pepper.
- Place an 18-inch-long length of wax paper on the counter. Put the flour in a shallow bowl and lightly dredge the chicken pieces in the flour, shaking off any excess. Put the chicken on the wax paper; reserve the 1 teaspoon remaining flour to use later.

• Heat a large nonstick skillet over medium-high heat. Add 1/2 tablespoon of the butter and 1 teaspoon of the olive oil to the pan and swirl the pan until the butter has melted. Add the chicken and cook until slightly golden on both sides, about 3 minutes per side. Transfer to a baking dish and place in the oven to keep warm.

• Add the remaining 1/2 tablespoon butter and 1 teaspoon olive oil to the skillet. Add the garlic and shallots and cook until soft and golden, about 2 minutes. Add the mushrooms, season with 1/8 teaspoon salt and a pinch of black pepper, and cook, stirring occasionally, until golden, about 5 minutes. Sprinkle in the reserved 1 teaspoon of flour and cook, stirring, for about 30 seconds. Add the Marsala wine, chicken broth, and parsley.

• Cook, stirring and scraping up any browned bits from the bottom of the pan with a wooden spoon, until thickened, about 2 minutes.

• Return the chicken to the skillet with the mushrooms, reduce heat to low, cover, and simmer in the sauce to let the flavors blend, about 4 to 5 minutes.

• To serve, put a piece of chicken on each of 4 serving plates. Spoon the mushrooms and sauce evenly over the top, and serve hot.

Chicken And Lemon Tagine

Ingredients

• 1 tbs olive oil

• 1 onion, finely chopped

• 2 garlic cloves, crushed or grated

• 1 carrot, finely diced

• 1 celery stalk, finely diced

• 1/4 tsp ground ginger

• 1/4 tsp ground turmeric

• 1 tsp ground cumin

• 1 tsp ground coriander

• 1/4 tsp ground cinnamon

• 600g boneless chicken thighs, diced

• 400g can diced tomatoes

• 400g can chickpeas, drained and rinsed

• 1 bay leaf

• 1/4 tsp salt

- Finely grated zest of 1 lemon
- 2 cups (370g) couscous
- Pinch of dried chilli flakes
- 100g plain or Greek yoghurt
- Fresh coriander, to serve

Instruction

- Heat the olive oil in a saucepan and fry the onion, garlic, carrot and celery. Add a little water (1-2 tbs) and cook for 10 minutes.
- Add the spices and cook, stirring, for 2 minutes. Add the chicken and cook until browned, then add the tomato and chickpeas, and enough water to cover the meat, followed by the bay leaf, then season with salt and pepper. Bring to the boil and simmer for 30 minutes.
- Add the lemon zest to the tagine and adjust the seasoning if required. If you've doubled the recipe, split the mixture in two and allow the extra meal to cool to room temperature. Refrigerate overnight before freezing for later use.
- Half-fill a saucepan with water and bring it to the boil. Place couscous in a bowl, add 3/4 cup (180ml)

boiling water and stir with a fork until all water is absorbed and the grains have separated.

• Tip the couscous into a sieve, place on the pan of boiling water (don't let it touch the water), cover and steam for 5-10 minutes until fluffy.

• Sprinkle tagine with dried chilli flakes, serve with couscous and yoghurt, and top with coriander.

Easy Bbq Chicken Pizza

Ingredients

• 1 ball of pizza dough or 1 prepared pizza crust

• 1/2-1 cup BBQ sauce

• 1 cup cooked chicken, cut in small cubes

• 2 cups shredded mozzarella cheese

• 1 cup shredded cheddar cheese

• 1 small green bell pepper, chopped

• 1/4 cup red onion or 3-4 green onions, finely chopped

• 1/4 cup chopped fresh cilantro

For Preparing The Pizza Dough

• Cornmeal, flour and extra-virgin olive oil

Instructions

• Place a pizza stone on the middle rack of the oven and preheat the oven to 500 for 25-30 minutes.

• Place a large piece of parchment paper on your rolling surface and sprinkle it with some cornmeal. Sprinkle some flour on your hands and place the dough on the prepared surface. Use your hands to gently shape the dough into a large round pizza circle, adding more flour if necessary to keep it from sticking. Then dough should be pretty even all around, but you can leave some extra dough on the edges for a crust.

• Brush the outer edge of the pizza with some olive oil.

• Add the BBQ sauce to the center of the pizza and use a spoon to evenly spread it across, leaving a little bit of room at the edge for the crust.

• Sprinkle the mozzarella and cheddar cheese evenly over the BBQ sauce then add the pepper, onion and chicken.

• Carefully transfer the pizza on the parchment paper to the preheated pizza stone.

• Bake at 500 for 8-12 minutes, depending on the thickness of your crust. The pizza is ready when the cheese is melted and the crust is golden brown.

• Carefully slide the pizza and parchment paper onto a cutting board and slice the pizza. Sprinkle with chopped fresh cilantro and serve.

Coconut Crusted Chicken Strips

Ingredients

• 2 boneless, skinless chicken breasts;

• 1/2 cup (or less) coconut flour;

• 2 eggs;

• A splash of full-fat coconut milk;

• 1 cup (more or less) shredded coconut;

• Sea salt and freshly cracked black pepper to taste;

• Coconut Crusted Chicken Strips Preparation

Preparation

• Preheat your oven to 400 F.

• Using a heavy object, like a rolling pin, hammer the chicken breasts so that they flatten to an even thickness. Cut the chicken into long strips that are about 3/4" to 1" in width.

• You will need three bowls; one for the coconut flour, one for the coconut milk and egg mixture (just beat the eggs and milk together) and one for the shredded coconut.

• Coat each chicken strip in the coconut flour, then dunk in the egg and coconut milk mixture and finally coat in the shredded coconut. When finished, place the chicken strips on a large baking sheet, leaving some space between each strip and cook for 10 to 12 minutes, or until chicken has completely cooked through.

• Serve with some paleo ketchup or a homemade plum or chilli sauce and enjoy

Quick Chicken Pho

Ingredients

• 3/4-inch (2 cm) section ginger

• 2 medium-large green onions

• 1 very small (.5 oz | 15 g) bunch cilantro sprigs

• 1 1/2 teaspoons coriander seeds

• 1 whole clove

• 3 1/2 to 4 cups (840 ml to 1 l) low-sodium chicken broth

- 2 cups (480 ml) water

- 6 to 8 ounces (180 to 225 g) boneless, skinless chicken breast or thighs

- About 1/2 teaspoon fine sea salt

- 5 ounces (150 g) dried narrow flat rice noodles

- 2 to 3 teaspoons fish sauce

- About 1/2 teaspoon organic sugar, or 1 teaspoon maple syrup (optional)

- Pepper (optional)

- Optional extras: Bean sprouts, mint sprigs, Thai basil, cilantro leaves, lime wedges, thinly-sliced chili peppers

Instructions

- Prepare the broth ingredients: Peel then slice the ginger into 4 or 5 coins. Smack with the flat side of a knife or meat mallet; set aside. Thinly slice the green parts of the green onion to yield 2 to 3 tablespoons; set aside for garnish. Cut the leftover sections into pinkie-finger lengths, bruise, then add to the ginger.

• Coarsely chop the leafy tops of the cilantro to yield 2 tablespoons; set aside for garnish. Set the remaining cilantro sprigs aside.

• Toast the broth ingredients: In a 3- to 4-quart (3 to 4 l) pot, toast the coriander seeds and clove over medium heat until fragrant, 1 to 2 minutes. Add the ginger and green onion sections. Stir for about 30 seconds, until aromatic.

• Add the broth and bring to a simmer: Slide the pot off heat, wait 15 seconds or so to briefly cool, then pour in the broth.

• Return the pot to the burner, then add the water, cilantro sprigs, chicken, and salt. Bring to a boil over high heat, then lower the heat to gently simmer.

• Remove the chicken from the broth once cooked: After 5 to 10 minutes of simmering, the chicken should be firm and cooked through (press on it and it should slightly yield).

• Continue to simmer the broth without the chicken for another 15 to 20 minutes (for a total of 30 minutes simmering time).

• Shred the chicken: Transfer the chicken to a bowl, flush with cold water to arrest the cooking, then drain. Let cool, then cut or shred into bite-size pieces. Cover loosely to prevent drying.

• Soak the rice noodles in hot water until pliable and opaque. Drain, rinse, and set aside.

• Strain the broth: When the broth is done, pour it through a fine-mesh strainer positioned over a 2-quart (2-liter) pot; line the strainer with muslin for superclear broth. Discard the solids. You should have about 4 cups.

• Finish the pho: Bring the strained broth to a boil over high heat. Put the noodles in a noodle strainer or mesh sieve and dunk in the hot broth to heat and soften, 5 to 60 seconds. Lift the noodles from the pot and divide between the 2 bowls. [Emma's note: I didn't find it necessary to soften my noodles any further. I just added them to the bowls and poured the hot broth over top. However, dunking them in the broth would make them more flavorful]

Basic Chicken Baby Puree
Ingredients

• 1 8-ounce boneless skinless chicken breast or thighs cubed

• 1 cup chicken stock low sodium

• 1 tsp dried parsley

Instructions

• In a medium saucepan, bring the cubed chicken, broth and parsley to a boil over medium heat. Turn heat down to low and simmer, covered, for 15-20 minutes or until chicken is just cooked through. Let cool slightly.

• Transfer all of the ingredients into a blender or food processor and puree until you reach your desired consistency, adding more stock in 1/4 cup increments if needed.

Slow Cooker Chicken and Rice Soup

Ingredients

• 3 chicken breasts, trimmed of fat and cut in half

• 1 cup parboiled rice (also called converted rice)

• 1 small onion, chopped

• 3 carrots, chopped

• 3 celery stalks, chopped

• 3 garlic cloves, minced

- 3 teaspoons salt

- Pepper to taste

- 2 teaspoons parsley

- 1 teaspoon thyme

- 1/2 teaspoon rosemary

- 1/2 teaspoon sage

- 1 bay leaf

- 2 tablespoons butter, optional

- 9 cups chicken broth

Instructions

- Place all ingredients in order in a slow cooker.

- Cook on low for 4 hours.

- A few minutes before serving, remove the chicken from slow cooker and shred or cut into cubes.

- Return chicken to the slow cooker, and let it cook for 5-10 more minutes.

- Alternate method

- If you prefer brown rice or wild rice, leave the parboiled rice out of the slow cooker when adding the other ingredients. While the soup is cooking in the slow cooker, prepare 1 cup uncooked brown or wild rice according to the package directions (once cooked, this will yield approximately 3 cups of rice). Stir the cooked rice into the soup just before serving.

Ingredients

• 700 g chicken breast diced

• 150 g cashews or almonds, raw (optional - omit for nut free)

• 300 g cream or coconut cream

• 50 g honey

• 1 bunch fresh coriander chopped

Marinade:-

• ½ Tbsp salt

• ¼-½ tsp chilli powder

• 1 tsp garam masala

• Optional: 1 tsp liquid tandoori colouring OR ¼ tsp red food colouring and 2 drops of yellow food colouring

• 10 g ginger

• 1 clove garlic peeled

• 15 g apple cider vinegar

Tomato paste:-

- 2 clove garlic
- 10 g ginger
- 30 g apple cider vinegar
- 400 g tin of Ardmona chopped tomatoes
- 100 g tomato paste
- Gravy:-
- 200 g brown onions peeled, halved
- 125 g butter
- 1 stick cinnamon
- 3 cloves
- 5 cardamom pods bruised
- 1 star anise
- 1 tsp cumin powder
- 1 tsp smoked paprika
- 1 tsp garam masala pepper free
- Metric - Imperial

Instructions

- Add nuts to mixer bowl, mill 10 sec/speed 9/MC on. Set aside.
- Without washing the bowl, (change to blunt blades for bellini and use speed 1 instead of reverse) add marinade ingredients to mixer bowl. Blend for 2

sec/speed 9/MC on. Scrape bowl down and repeat 3 times.

• Add the chicken and stir through marinade for 10 sec/speed 2/reverse/MC on. Scrape mixer bowl out completely, set aside in a separate bowl to allow chicken to marinate.

• Without washing the bowl, add tomato paste ingredients to mixer bowl. Blend 1 min/speed 8/MC on. Set tomato paste aside in a separate bowl again.

• Without washing the bowl, add onions to mixer bowl and chop 5 sec/speed 5/MC on. Scrape bowl down.

• Add 60 g or 2.1 oz butter to mixer bowl, cook 10 min/100°C or 212°F/speed 2/butterfly/MC on.

• Add remaining butter (65 g or 2.3 oz), cinnamon, whole cloves, cardamom, star anise, cumin and paprika to mixer bowl.

• Cook 5 min/100°C or 212°F/slowest speed/reverse/butterfly/MC on.

• Add reserved tomato paste mixture, garam masala and 2 tsp salt to mixer bowl. Cook for 4 min/steaming temperature/slowest speed/reverse/butterfly/MC on.

• Add reserved marinated chicken mixture to mixer bowl. Cook for 12 min/100°C or 212°F/slowest speed/reverse/butterfly/MC on.

• Add reserved nut meal, cream and honey to mixer bowl. Cook for 4 min/100°C or 212°F/slowest speed/reverse/butterfly/MC on. While cooking, use your spatula to stir the curry occasionally.

• Pour curry into an insulated server, remove whole spices, stir through chopped coriander and let it sit covered for 10 min.

Chimichurri

Ingredients

• 1/2 cup minced, packed cilantro or parsley (or a mix of both)

• 6 tablespoons red wine vinegar

• 2 tablespoons olive oil

• 2 cloves garlic, minced (2 teaspoons)

• 1/2 teaspoon dried oregano

• 1/4 teaspoon salt

• 1/4 – 1/2 teaspoon crushed red pepper flakes, depending on your taste for the hot'n'spicy

• Optional: 1/4 cup minced onion (white, yellow, red, or shallots)

Instructions

• Combine all ingredients and let stand at room temperature for at least 10 minutes and up to 2 hours before serving.

• This will keep refrigerated up to 48 hours. Makes about 3/4 cup of sauce.

Melt In Your Mouth (MIYM) Chicken Breasts

Ingredients:

• 1 cup sour cream

• 2 teaspoons garlic powder

• 1 teaspoon seasoned salt

• 1/2 teaspoon fresh ground black pepper

• 1 1/2 cups freshly grated Parmesan cheese, divided

• 3 pounds boneless chicken breasts, trimmed of excess fat

Instructions:

- Preheat oven to 375°F. Lightly coat a 9×13 baking dish with nonstick spray and set aside.
- In a medium bowl, mix together the sour cream, garlic powder, seasoned salt, pepper, and 1 cup of Parmesan cheese.
- Place the chicken breasts evenly into the pan. Spread the sour cream mixture on top of the chicken. Sprinkle with the remaining Parmesan cheese.
- Bake for 25-30 minutes, or until the chicken is cooked through.
- Turn the oven to broil and place the pan under the broiler for 2-3 minutes until lightly browned on top.
- Serve immediately.

Mustard and Mushroom Chicken

Ingredients

- 2 tablespoons Butter
- 2 cloves Garlic, minced
- 3 tablespoons Flour
- 1 cup Chicken Stock
- 1/2 cup Milk
- 3-4 tablespoons Mustard

- 1 tablespoon Tarragon

- 2 tablespoons Olive Oil

- 8 ounces sliced Mushrooms

- 3 tablespoons White Wine

- 1 Yellow Onion, chopped

- 2 pounds Chicken Breasts

- Flour to dredge the chicken

- Salt and Pepper

Instructions

- Preheat your oven to 300 degrees. Prepare the chicken by cutting each chicken breast in half and then pounding it with a meat mallet until it has a thin and even thickness.

- Then start preparing the sauce. Start by melting the butter in a medium saucepan. Stir in the garlic, and let it cook for one minute and then stir in the flour. Stir for another minute. Then slowly add the chicken stock and milk whisk until the butter/flour mixture is completely incorporated. Then bring to a slow boil. Let boil for 1 minute, stirring frequently. This lets the sauce thicken. Then add in the mustard and tarragon. Go ahead and add extra mustard if you really like mustard. Set the sauce aside.

• Heat 1 tablespoon of olive oil in a skillet over medium heat. Add the mushrooms and toss in the olive oil. Sprinkle with salt and pepper. Saute the mushrooms for 4 minutes, and then add the white wine and the onions. Let saute for another 4 minutes. Then add the mushrooms and onions to the sauce.

• In a bowl combine about 1/2 cup flour and 1/2 teaspoon of both salt and pepper. Using the same skillet, heat another tablespoon of olive oil over medium-high heat. Once the skillet is hot, dredge the chicken in the flour and place in the skillet. It will only take a couple minutes to brown on each side. Place the browned chicken in a casserole dish. Continue to brown the chicken in batches, adding more olive oil to the pan as necessary.

• Once all of the chicken has browned, pour the sauce over, and place it in the oven to bake for 45 minutes.

Ingredients

• 4 Boneless Skinless Chicken Breasts

• 4 ounces of Cream Cheese cut into bite chunks (not whipped)

• 4 Jalapenos

• 1/2 cup Shredded Cheddar Cheese

• 8 slices of Bacon

Instructions

• Start by heating your oven to 300 degrees and then get to chopping the jalapenos. If you like hot spicy heat – leave the seeds. If you want a mild heat, remove the seeds.

• Then move on to pounding out the chicken breasts until they are quite thin. You want them to double in size. Cover the chicken in plastic wrap, and place on a strong surface and use a meat mallet or a cast iron pan to pound them out.

• Next, place a long thin chunk of cream cheese in the center.

• Add jalapeno and cheddar cheese on top, and then wrap the chicken around it.

• Use 2 slices of bacon to wrap around each chicken breast sealing it shut. Sprinkle with salt and pepper.

• Place the bacon wrapped chicken breasts in a baking sheet lined with aluminum foil.

• After 45 minutes, remove the chicken from the oven, and drain any bacon fat off the pan.

• Increase the oven temperature to 400 degrees, letting the bacon crisp up for another 10 minutes or as long as necessary.

20 Minute Sesame Chicken

Ingredients

• 1.5 pounds Boneless Skinless Chicken Breast

• 3 tablespoons All Purpose Flour

• 3 teaspoons Sesame Oil

• 3/4 cup Low Sodium Soy Sauce

• 3 cloves of Garlic pressed or minced

• 1 teaspoon Peeled Fresh Ginger grated

• 1/2 teaspoon - 1 teaspoon Sriracha to taste

• 2 teaspoons Corn Starch

• 2 cups Sliced Mushrooms

• 1 cup Snow Peas

• 1/2 cup Shredded Carrot I get it from the grocery store salad bar

• 2 teaspoons Sesame Seeds

Instructions

• Serve with your favorite rice (I used Uncle Ben's Brown and Wild Rice Mix)

• First, use a knife or kitchen sheers to cut the chicken up into pieces that are about 2 bites big.

• Then toss the chicken in the flour, until it is evenly coated in flour. Next heat a teaspoon of sesame oil in a wok or skillet over medium heat. Once hot, add 1/3 of the chicken, and cook each side for 2 minutes, until browned. Then cook the rest of the chicken in two more batches, adding another teaspoon of sesame oil to the pan each time. Set the cooked chicken aside in a bowl.

• Whisk the soy sauce, garlic, ginger, sriracha, and corn starch together and then pour it into the same wok or skillet over medium heat. Add the mushrooms, and let cook for 3 minutes, stirring frequently.

• Add the chicken, and stir to coat it in the sauce. Cook for another 4 minutes. Lastly, add the snow peas, carrot, and sesame seeds. Cook for 2 minutes. (I used this time to make my Uncle Ben's microwaveable rice).

Classic Pot Roast

Ingredients

• 16 ounces Chuck Roast

• 1 ½ cup Sliced Mushrooms

• 1 packed Dry Onion Soup Mix

• 2 10.5 ounce Cans of Cream of Mushroom Soup

• Egg Noodles

Instructions

• Place the beef in a casserole dish or dutch oven. Pour the mushrooms, dry onion soup mix, and cream of mushroom soup over. Fill one of the empty soup cans with water and pour it over the beef. Make sure that the liquid submerges the beef. Add extra soup and water if necessary.

• Cover the dish and place it in the oven set to 225 degrees. Let roast for 4 ½ hours, or until the beef is so tender it is falling apart. Serve over egg noodles.

Chicken with a Sherry Mushroom Sauce

Ingredients

• 4 Chicken Breasts

• Salt and Pepper

• 2 tablespoons Butter

• 2 cloves of Garlic crushed or chopped

• 8 ounces Sliced Mushrooms I like baby bella

• 1 cup Dry Sherry

• 1/3 cup Heavy Cream

• 1/2 teaspoon Thyme

Instructions

• Heat your oven to 350 degrees.

• Melt 1 tablespoon of butter in a large skillet over medium-high heat. Generously salt and pepper both sides of the chicken breasts. Once the butter has melted, add the chicken to the skillet. Then add 1/4 cup of sherry. Cook the chicken for 3 minutes per side, until browned. Then remove the chicken from the skillet and place it on a plate while you work on the sauce.

• Melt another tablespoon of butter in the same skillet you just used to cook the chicken. Add the garlic and stir, scraping up any brown bits. After a minute add the mushrooms. Generously salt and pepper and toss until the mushrooms are evenly coated with butter. Cook for 2 minutes. Then add the remaining sherry. Let the mushrooms simmer for another 4 minutes. Then stir in the cream and thyme. Let the sauce reduce for 5 minutes then add the chicken back to the skillet. Place the skillet in the oven for 30 minutes so that the chicken can finish cooking. (Make sure you are using an oven-safe skillet!)

• After 30 minutes in the oven the chicken should be done - serve it with pasta or rice pilaf. Spoon the sauce over the top.

Andhra Style Chicken Curry

Ingredients

• 3 Tbsp Refined oil

• 1 Bay leaf

• 3 Green cardamom

• 3 Cloves

• 1 small Cinnamon stick

• 1 Onion, sliced

- 1 tbsp Ginger-garlic paste

- 1/2 kg Chicken (cut into bite size pieces)

- 1 tsp Turmeric

- to taste Salt

- 2 cups Water

- 2 Green chillies (slit)

- Handful Curry leaves

- 2 tsp Red chilli powder

- 2 tbsp Cashew nuts - poppy seed paste (Soak 15 cashews and 1 Tbsp poppy seed in a cup of milk for an hour. Grind it into a paste.)

- 2 tsp Chicken masala

- 2 tsp Kasoori methi

- 1 tsp Garam masala

- 2 tsp Dhaniya powder

- To garnish Coriander leaves, chopped

Instructions

- In a wok add refined oil. Add a bay leaf, green cardamom, cloves, cinnamon. Let them release the aroma.

• Now add onions. Saute till golden brown and then add the ginger-garlic paste. Mix and add the chicken pieces. Saute till they start to color a bit.

• Now add the turmeric and salt. Toss and add water.

• Add the green chilli and curry leaves. Let the curry simmer.

• Add the red chilli powder, cashew nut -poppy seed paste, chicken masala, kasoori methi, garam masala and dhaniya powder. Mix well and let the curry simmer till the chicken is cooked. Add more water if required.

• Garnish with coriander leaves and serve with steamed rice.

Healthy Butter Chicken

Ingredients

• 1 tbs unsalted butter

• 500g chicken thigh (roughly chopped)

• 1 onion (finely sliced)

• 1 large garlic clove (crushed)

• 2 tsp ginger (freshly grated)

• 1 tsp cumin

- 2 tsp garam masala
- 1/2 tsp cardamom
- 1 tbs coriander (finely chopped)
- 1 tin canned diced tomato
- 3/4 cup massel chicken style liquid stock
- 1/2 cup low-fat greek yoghurt
- 1/4 cup low-fat thickened cream
- 2 cups steamed rice
- Coriander leaves (to garnish)

Instructions

- Heat a large non-stick frying pan on medium and add half the butter.
- Onions add bursts of flavour to any meal. Here's how to properly chop them.
- Add chicken and onion and brown for a couple of minutes.
- Remove mixture from the pan and set aside.
- Reduce heat to low and add remaining butter as well as the garlic, ginger, cumin, garam marsala, cardamom and coriander.
- Cook for 1-2 minutes before returning chicken to the pan, along with the tomatoes and chicken stock.

• Increase the heat and bring to the boil.

• Reduce heat and simmer for 10 minutes before adding yoghurt and cream.

• Heat through and serve on rice garnished with coriander leaves.

Creamy Avocado And Spinach Pasta

Ingredients

• 10 oz spaghetti dry, or fettuccine, I used semolina pasta

• 1 clove garlic

• 1 avocado

• 1 cup spinach fresh

• 1/2 cup pecans

• 1/4 cup basil

• 1/4 cup Parmesan cheese grated

• 1 tbsp lemon juice freshly squeezed

• 3/4 to 1 cup pasta water

• 1/2 tsp salt or to taste

• 1/2 tsp pepper or to taste

Instructions

• Cook pasta: Cook the pasta according to the package instructions.

• Make the avocado sauce: Add the rest of the ingredients to your blender and blend until it turns into a smooth sauce. Start with 3/4 cup of pasta water and add more as needed to get the consistency you want.

• Assemble: Toss the pasta with the sauce in a bowl and serve immediately. This sauce is best served the day it is made, as it uses avocados which will turn a brownish color.

Chicken Salad

Ingredients

For The Salad:

• 1 pound boneless, skinless (raw) chicken breasts, cut into 2 1/2-inch chunks (or 2 to 3 cups cooked chicken meat)

• 2 stalks celery, chopped

• 1/2 red bell pepper, seeded and chopped

• 4 to 6 green olives, pitted and minced

• 1/4 cup chopped red onion

• 1/2 to 1 whole apple, cored and chopped

• 1/3 head iceberg head lettuce, sliced and chopped

For The Dressing:

- 5 tablespoons mayonnaise
- 1 tablespoon plum preserves, or any sweet berry preserve (or a lesser amount of honey)
- 2 teaspoons fresh squeezed lemon juice
- Salt and pepper to taste

Instructions

- Poach the chicken (skip if using already cooked chicken): Bring a pot with 2 quarts of well salted water (1 tablespoon salt) to a boil. Add the chicken breast (cut into large chunks) and return the water to a simmer. Then turn off the heat, and cover the pot. Let the chicken sit for 15 minutes (time it) or more while you prepare everything else.
- Make the dressing: Prepare the chicken salad dressing in a large bowl. Mix together the mayonnaise, preserves, and lemon juice. Taste for the proper balance of sweetness and acidity. The salad dressing should not be too sweet, nor too sour.
- Add more preserves or lemon juice until you have reached the balance you want. Add salt and pepper to taste.

• Mix in the chopped celery, bell pepper, olives, red onion, and apple.

• Dice the chicken, mix with dressing and vegetables: Remove the chicken from the poaching water and dice it. (Or dice already cooked chicken if that is what you are using for this salad.) Mix it in with the dressing and vegetables.

• Add lettuce: At this point you can make ahead. When ready to serve, fold in the sliced and chopped iceberg lettuce.

Classic Chicken Pot Pie

Ingredients

Crust

• 1 box Pillsbury refrigerated pie crusts, softened as directed on box

Filling

• 1/3 cup butter or margarine

• 1/3 cup chopped onion

• 1/3 cup all-purpose flour

• ½ teaspoon salt

• ¼ teaspoon pepper

- 1 ¾ cups Progresso chicken broth (from 32-oz carton)
- ½ cup milk
- 2 ½ cups shredded cooked chicken or turkey
- 2 cups frozen mixed vegetables, thawed

Instructions

- Prevent your screen from going dark while you cook.
- Heat oven to 425°F. Prepare pie crusts as directed on box for Two-Crust Pie using 9-inch glass pie pan.
- In 2-quart saucepan, melt butter over medium heat. Add onion; cook 2 minutes, stirring frequently, until tender. Stir in flour, salt and pepper until well blended. Gradually stir in broth and milk, cooking and stirring until bubbly and thickened.
- Stir in chicken and mixed vegetables. Remove from heat. Spoon chicken mixture into crust-lined pan. Top with second crust; seal edge and flute. Cut slits in several places in top crust.
- Bake 30 to 40 minutes or until crust is golden brown. During last 15 to 20 minutes of baking,

cover crust edge with strips of foil to prevent excessive browning. Let stand 5 minutes before serving.